Forev

Anyone who values honest, res[has ample reason to be concerned abou. ... ..aini or public and private discourse today. At all levels of society, we now witness communication practices that would have been unthinkable in the recent past:

- Government leaders substitute scare tactics and bullying for thoughtful policy analysis and consensus building.
- Senior executives of our leading businesses engage in outright fraud and deception, harming customers, investors and other important stakeholders.
- Many institutions that serve the public good—such as schools and hospitals—struggle to articulate their mission in the face of rising costs and increasing market pressures.
- Families, trying to engage in shared activities, find themselves easily distracted by the ubiquitous smart phone.

At all levels, our society depends upon healthy communication practices in order to function. Unfortunately, many of our communication practices are unhealthy, and our communities suffer as a result.

Human communication is first of all an *ethical* enterprise. The values we actually live by are displayed vividly through the ways we communicate with each other. Honest and healthy communication rests on shared values, which are the glue that binds people together. Such values as respecting others, honoring truth, avoiding doing harm and promoting the common good are among the bedrock values that support constructive dialogue. Moreover, these values are what make authentic community possible.

Alongside values, a set of practices forms the foundation for healthy communication. First is expressing our views in a spirit of reasonable cooperation. The best conversations are mutually beneficial collaborations, not fights. Next is providing good reasons for our views. Traditionally, the best reasons are grounded in verifiable facts. Third is attentive listening to opposing views. Those who point out exceptions to our ideas help us move closer to the truth and deserve our respectful attention.

1

The authors of this book understand the critical role of underlying ethical values in our communication practices. The spirit of cooperation and respectful engagement appears on every page that follows. This alone qualifies *#CanWeTalk* as an important remedy to the illness that weakens so much of our communication today. Another important feature of this book makes it truly stand out: It is crystal clear in its exploration of the complex dynamics of communication. Anyone who reads this book will grow as a communicator because this book helpfully removes any mystery about skills like active listening and responding to others.

#CanWeTalk is based on relevant scholarly work. Even though this is not an "academic" textbook, its information is solid, drawing upon prior substantial research. At the same time, it is entirely accessible and practical. These two features of this book—its scholarly grounding and practical relevance—are reflective of the qualities of the authors themselves. Peter McDermott and Diana Hulse bring a refreshing combination of extensive real-world experience and serious scholarly acumen. Their shared credentials in law enforcement and counselor education provide a strikingly unique perspective. When I observed them working with police personnel and university students, I was struck by their fresh and engaging approach, which puts everyone at ease and promotes significant learning. This book exemplifies the best of their approach: Reading it is almost like interacting with Peter and Diana face-to-face.

It has been a genuine privilege for me to work with Peter and Diana in their roles with the Waide Center for Applied Ethics at Fairfield University, where I have watched them cultivate the ideas and methods that appear in this book. Our society deeply needs this book, which could not have come at a better time.

David P. Schmidt, Ph.D.
Director
The Patrick J. Waide Center for Applied Ethics
Fairfield University

Table of Contents

Acknowledgements

Our book project, focused on the active listening and responding skills for face-to-face interactions and the competencies needed to build interpersonal relationships, succeeded because of a network of relationships and sustained support from many people.

Our first thanks goes to Dr. David Schmidt, Associate Professor of Business Ethics and Director of the Patrick J. Waide Center for Applied Ethics at Fairfield University. Both of us are connected to the Center's work and David served as the mentor and major impetus behind our decision to write this book. His generosity of spirit and trust in our abilities, as seen in his beautifully written foreword, are evidence of his desire to see our work in print and available to a wide range of readers.

We received ongoing support from Dr. Bob Hannafin, Dean of the Graduate School of Education and Allied Professions (GSEAP) and from Lynn Holforty, Program Coordinator for GSEAP, who expertly edited our manuscript and cheered us on. Thanks also go to the Graduate Assistants in the Counselor Education Department, Erica Guzzardi and Jillian Noto, who tirelessly revised, revamped, re-formatted, and provided feedback on ways to make our book content attractive and useful to contemporary audiences.

We also appreciate the enthusiastic support of Susan Cipollaro, Associate Director of Media Relations and Content Marketing at Fairfield University, who inspired a title that captures the attention of those we wish to reach.

Rounding out our network of relationships are the illustrations by Truman Hatfield of Valley Glen, CA. Truman was approached by his grandmother (Diana) to see if he might use his skill set to visually present the dilemmas we address in major sections of the book. Truman's perceptive grasp of the book's intent led to three significant illustrations that enhance our message.

We thank all our friends and colleagues who join us in the quest for more civility and competence in interpersonal conversations and personal relationships at home, at work, and across daily interactions in our society.

And finally, we thank each other for having faith in our message and in one another to trust the process and complete this project.

Diana Hulse and Peter J. McDermott; January 2019

About the Authors

#CanWeTalk represents the most recent collaboration between Diana Hulse, Professor and Chair of the Counselor Education Department at Fairfield University and Peter J. McDermott, Distinguished Visiting Professional in the Patrick J. Waide Center for Applied Ethics at Fairfield University.

Diana Hulse's 40 years as a counselor and counselor educator include teaching and research interests in group work training and practice, corrective feedback exchange in group settings, and counseling supervision. She is the author of the Corrective Feedback Instrument-Revised (CFI-R) featured in this Guide.

Peter McDermott, with 48 years in law enforcement, is a retired captain from the West Hartford and Windsor Connecticut Police Departments and a retired instructor from the Connecticut Police Academy in Meriden, Connecticut.

Together Hulse and McDermott have published a handbook and several articles in the *FBI Law Enforcement Bulletin*, *The Police Chief*, and *Counseling Today* on the topics of interpersonal skills training, skills for feedback exchange, and skills for facilitating leadership tasks. In 2016 they were lead instructors for a pioneering training series on active listening and responding skills for police personnel on the Fairfield University campus.

Introduction

Interpersonal relationships are essential to human existence, not unlike air and water. Interpersonal, face-to-face exchanges allow people to develop bonds whether for minutes or for life, to advance associations of long-term value or encounters with brief social satisfaction. The more individuals learn ways to build respectful, meaningful, and pleasing relationships the healthier everyone becomes.

Technological progress offers humans many options today to interact with and stay connected to others. Although valuable, the widespread use of technology is diffusing the significance of face-to-face communication and as a result, generating a huge gap in people's ability to call forth necessary skills to engage in civil face-to-face exchanges. A strong ethical obligation exists to close this gap and build interpersonal competencies so that humans can thrive.

Since the mid-1990s to the current day, a number of writers have referenced the need for face-to-face interactions and the skills to listen to and understand others. In 2008 Cacioppo and Patricin encouraged people to strengthen love and social connections, which they say are necessary in life. Cacioppo concedes that humans can survive in society with technology, but later may come to regret missed chances to build and maintain satisfying interpersonal relationships.

Lown (1996) and Joseph (2016) lament the fact that healing is now replaced by treating, resulting in more impersonal and transactional doctor-patient interactions. They call upon the medical profession to train its personnel in the skills of listening and communicating with others.

Citing an increasing gulf between the police and the public, McDermott and Hulse (2016) appeal to law enforcement to train their personnel in the necessary interpersonal skills that will ultimately help close the police-public divide. Rogers' discussion in *The Harvard Business Review* (2018) about respect in the workplace fits naturally with the need for higher levels of interpersonal competencies.

Dyson's vivid account of Robert F. Kennedy's meeting with black individuals more than 50 years ago illuminates the continued importance of listening skills. The meeting Dyson describes "taught Kennedy a valuable lesson about listening to what you don't want to hear" (2018 p. 267).

The purpose of *#CanWeTalk* is to shine a spotlight on basic active listening and responding skills which are the pathway for developing and improving discourse at home, at school, in social, church, medical, and work settings, and in everyday contacts in stores and banks, restaurants, and with law enforcement personnel.

Recurring examples of interpersonal conflicts in our society over ethical failures, gender discrimination, and cultural bias have focused the public's attention on de-escalation strategies and other attempts to respond to physical and verbal tensions. However, in order for de-escalation to succeed, one first needs a basic command of active listening and responding skills to attend wholeheartedly to another person, to build an understanding of that person's opinion, and to eventually gain and express empathy for that person's perspective.

Listening and talking are our most valuable skills. Once people get the sense that someone is not listening to them, it is hard to correct that impression. Active listening and responding skills help people find the words they often cannot retrieve when they want to lessen a painful situation for a friend or family member. Sometimes just the act of active listening can be all a person needs to do to ease tension and offer support to others.

Proficiency in verbal and non-verbal active listening and responding skills helps individuals pinpoint which skills they need in the moment to achieve a desired objective. When and why, for example, is it important to use a calm voice tone to slow down a conversation in order to help individuals concentrate on what is most important to them? When might a reflection of co-workers' feelings help them feel heard and valued, and as a result decrease future negative actions on their part? Do clarifying and summarizing a child's comments help parents better communicate that they hear their child's concerns?

We must ask ourselves:

"Can I identify active listening and responding skills?

Have I ever learned what these skills are?

When was the last time I intentionally used these skills in my daily communications?"

You may have the tendency to say:

"I already do this; I already have these skills."

It is a common belief that active listening and responding skills just happen. If a person can speak, that person must have interpersonal skills. Often categorized as "soft" skills, this designation automatically diminishes their importance and value.

In reality, soft skills do not seem readily available to individuals or practiced by them in everyday interpersonal exchanges. Active listening and responding skills are in need of major revitalization that brings them front and center to their role in promoting civil discourse.

Readers of *#CanWeTalk* will learn and understand the function and value of verbal and non-verbal active listening and responding skills and ways to apply them in routine, daily interactions. Readers will also discover how to expand on these foundational skills to give and receive feedback and facilitate successful meetings and task groups. *Giving and receiving feedback* is a critically underused competency, missing in employment and social exchanges. *Facilitating successful group functions*, like meetings and team projects, is another undeveloped competency necessary to promote positive results in everyday work-related endeavors.

The time for constructive and civil interpersonal exchanges is now. Gaining competency in active listening and responding skills will make it possible for individuals to behave reflexively and intentionally, and to be present for others when needed, instead of looking back on missed opportunities to connect with others in significant ways.

There are going to be times in life when active listening and responding skills will be THE essential skills to use with a significant person, friend, sibling, colleague, parent, or child. That realization alone is worth the investment of time and effort to practice and refine the competencies for building and enhancing interpersonal relationships.

PART ONE

Basic Active Listening and Responding Skills

Beginning a Conversation

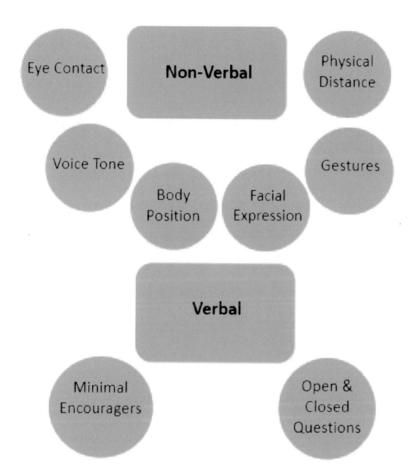

CHAPTER 1

Non-Verbal and Verbal Attending Skills to Begin Conversations

Non-verbal and verbal behaviors influence first impressions. One's engaging and welcoming non-verbal presentation and initial words can lead to successful, civil, and productive interactions. Conversely, tone of voice or a frown can noticeably influence another type of discourse. In this chapter, we organize the attending skills into two categories: *Non-verbal and verbal skills* that invite conversation. We provide a description of each skill and examples of its use. With this information, readers can recognize and assess their own competency level with each skill, and practice the skills in all kinds of face-to-face daily encounters at work, at home, at school, and with friends.

Non-Verbal Attending Skills

Eye Contact: In most cases, people initiate and maintain eye contact as a way to start a conversation. Learning one's own personal tendencies with eye contact is a first step to understanding how to use eye contact for specific and varied reasons.

Think about a time when the person you were talking with avoided eye contact. How did you feel? Did the lack of eye contact encourage you to talk or create a barrier? Did you judge the person for not showing eye contact? Suppose you are in a conversation with someone who is watching TV, reading an iPad; looking at a cell phone and saying, "I'm listening." How does that work for you? Even wearing sunglasses while trying to have a meaningful conversation sets up a message of "I'm really not listening." Does taking off one's sunglasses change the interaction for both the speaker and the listener?

Imagine you are with three friends at a table in a restaurant. You try to get their attention to discuss the afternoon plans. The three friends continue to verbally say "Okay, okay, okay…" but they are not looking up from their phones. Do these behaviors have an effect on how you continue the conversation?

Voice Tone: Tone of voice represents an attending behavior that immediately opens a conversation or forms a barrier that will be hard to surmount. Those in positions of authority, like bosses, doctors, teachers, supervisors, and police officers need to be aware of the power that their tone of voice can bring to an interpersonal encounter. Voice tone in combination with eye contact creates a lasting first impression. It is helpful to discern whether the purpose of the interaction is to converse, inquire, console, provide feedback, or apprehend.

People do not like someone yelling at, demeaning, or disrespecting them. Voice is the vehicle that often determines the success or failure of a conversation. Think of how many ways one can change the words, "thank you" with voice tone. Those words can come across as sincere or as an expression of anger or sarcasm.

Consider a meeting where the facilitator decided to use an authoritarian tone of voice to establish order and control of the meeting. Later when the meeting ends, the facilitator is surprised that others at the table did not interact as she expected. Would a change to a more engaging tone of voice have yielded different results?

Facial Expressions: Facial expressions evoke a variety of emotions and responses in the beholder. Think about how a smile, frown, or scowl can set the tone of an interaction. Depending on the purpose of the conversation, one may use a smile for reassurance or a more firm facial expression when correcting a mistake.

Learning how and when to alter facial expressions for specific purposes is an important skill to use with care and intention.

Congruence occurs when one's facial expressions match one's actual behavior. Mixed signals given by confusing voice tones and eye contact often lead to negative results. Reflect on a situation where a supervisor receives a complaint about rude and disrespectful behavior on the part of an employee. The employee explains to the supervisor, "All I said was, 'can I help you?'" The supervisor clarifies that the complaint had to do with eye contact and tone of voice when talking with the customer. The potential positive impact of the employee's words, "can I help you?" was erased by the employee's non-verbal behavior. The lesson here is that people will believe what they experience in one's facial expressions over the actual words delivered.

Body Position: This behavior in combination with attire, like police or medical uniforms, sets in motion an image of power. If a doctor wants to engage a patient, he or she can enter the consulting room displaying a relaxed body position. Similarly, law enforcement personnel who enter a room in uniform already communicate a position of command. Depending on the point of an interaction, a police officer can choose to counteract the uniform's impact with a more relaxed use of body position. In a seated situation, leaning in toward a person shows interest and invites dialogue.

A person's size and appearance enhances, or intimidates, turns on or turns off a conversation. Friendly orientation of the body towards people displays openness and a willingness to listen. Opening of arms and hands invites conversation. Depending on the purpose of the exchange, the listener can use body position to dominate or intimidate.

Gestures: In combination with the attending skills of eye contact, voice tone, facial expressions, and body position, a person's gestures add another level of information to influence the direction of an interpersonal exchange. A simple handshake communicates a welcoming expression that invites conversation.

To strengthen civil discourse one needs to be aware of all behaviors, including gestures. The gesture of waving one's hand asking, "Come here" is different from pointing a finger at somebody and indicating with the movement of the finger that the person should "come here." The purpose of both gestures is to bring the person closer, but each gesture has a different meaning and impact. Waving a hand to say hello is different than waving a fist. Sitting down in a conversation with folded arms signals a different message from opening one's arms and hands.

Physical Distance: Body proximity is a powerful tool that can express a calm and relaxed tone or in specific situations a threating tone. Learning to read the proximity needs of people engaged in conversation requires sensitivity to the other person's wishes and an understanding of the point of the conversation.

People vary in their comfort with physical closeness while conversing. Too close can feel threatening at worst and uncomfortable at best. Observing a person's non-verbal signals will help a listener choose the best physical distance. If the goal of the conversation is to engage someone's attention, then it is important to make that person comfortable. One person may feel comfortable with close proximity; another person may pull away.

Non-verbal attending skills are everyday skills that one can practice, develop, and evaluate. To strengthen skills when a family member or friend initiates a conversation, pay attention to the following:

Try direct eye contact with the person

Use a voice tone to encourage the person to talk

Use a welcoming facial expression and open hand gestures

Ongoing assessment of a conversation allows the listener to make adjustments to achieve the desired results for the conversation. Watch for the speaker's reactions in order to assess whether the attending non-verbal behaviors aid or shut down the conversation. Remember these are attending skills. The objective is to allow the speaker a climate of receptiveness where you, the listener can focus on what the speaker wants to you to hear.

Verbal Attending Skills

Combined with non-verbal attending behaviors are the verbal attending skills that complete this section on beginning a conversation.

Open Invitations to Talk: Verbal invitations help establish rapport with the person in the conversation. One of the goals of open invitations to talk is to draw out further information without being intrusive. To engage a child's description of an accident, one could say, "I am very interested in what you experienced. Can you tell me more about what you saw?

Minimal Encouragers: Short statements of "I see," "I hear you," "I'm with you," let people know that the listener is paying attention and wants to hear more. Minimal encouragers prompt more conversation with very slight interruption. Other examples include, "Yes" "Right" "Okay" "Hmm."

Open and Closed Questions: Generally *open questions* like, "can you give me an example," convey interest on the part of the listener to encourage and draw out more conversation. In situations where one person is reporting an event that requires urgent and concise information, the listener could ask a *closed question*, to obtain specific facts, "What was the color of the car?"

The Role of Non-Verbal and Verbal Attending Skills in Beginning a Conversation

As emphasized throughout this chapter, attending non-verbal and verbal skills are important to understand separately in order to appreciate the impact each has on human interactions. Common knowledge states that non-verbal behaviors reveal the most information and have the most impact in interpersonal exchanges. If people in authority want to increase their interpersonal connections with others, they need to review their non-verbal skills to figure out which ones need to be adjusted in order to achieve open communication. The bottom line is that people want to know that others are interested in what they have to say.

Using minimal encouragers assists the listener in drawing out messages that others want to share. In combination, non-verbal and verbal attending skills come together to promote positive and satisfying exchanges. Conversely, the misuse of non-verbal behaviors and the lack of verbal attending behaviors can lead to negativity and confusion, or simply end the conversation.

Building and Continuing a Conversation

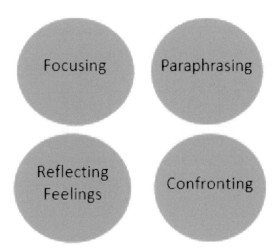

CHAPTER 2

Building and Continuing a Conversation with Active Responding Skills

Solidifying a welcoming tone to build and continue productive and respectful interactions comes with the application of *focusing, paraphrasing, reflecting feelings, and confronting*. These four active responding skills help a listener gain knowledge, gather information, and impart understanding and empathy to others. With knowledge of each skill's purpose and with practice of each skill, individuals can draw upon them at strategic points in all interactions, of both short and long durations (Okun & Kantrowitz, 2015; Young, 2017).

Focusing helps the listener gather information on relevant facts without cutting off the person; rather, the listener chooses to cut off unnecessary content in order to "hold the focus." This skill is helpful when the listener thinks that slowing down the tempo of the conversation to concentrate on one or two points helps the listener understand the person's story or message.

For example, when listening to a child tell about a difficult school day, the parent might say:

"Tom, you seem very upset about what happened today in science class. I want you to think about what specifically bothered you the most and tell me what that was."

This skill helps a listener draw out the most important and meaningful parts of the speaker's story.

When the goal is gathering information and evidence or getting to the most essential point in a conversation, focusing is a helpful tool. A coworker says:

"I couldn't find a parking spot so I missed the briefing session this morning. Somebody ought to do something about the parking situation. I can't find that memo and I'm not sure what to say to my boss when he calls me this afternoon."

One focusing response might be, "I sense there is a lot going on for you this morning. Can you tell me what is most important to you right now?"

In response to an employee suggestion, the supervisor says:

"I know this is a pretty detailed idea that you think could help the organization, but in order to move forward, I would first like to hear the budgetary implications of what you propose."

Paraphrasing represents an essential step toward expressing empathy to another person. Paraphrasing helps listeners gain a clear grasp of what a person is saying by repeating back important thoughts, behaviors, or intentions embedded in the speaker's statement. Paraphrasing does not pressure the person by asking a question. Paraphrasing is not simply "parroting" or repeating back the exact words. It is a short restatement in different words and without judgment which goes a long way in building trusting conversations.

A community resident approaches a police officer and says, "I have been living in this neighborhood for 30 years; when are the police going to do something about the speeding and disregard for residents?" The officer could offer the following, "You want the police to get more involved and pay attention to what's going on." In this paraphrase, the officer has noticed and repeated back what appears to be the real message.

Think of a paraphrase as a distilled version of a story. An employee says to a team leader:

"Well, I didn't mean to offend him. I am not saying 'Sorry' because he started it! He knows how to get me all riled up in a meeting and he does it on purpose."

A paraphrase could be:

"So, you admit that you knew your behavior was improper, but you are not going to apologize because he provoked you."

Reflecting Feelings builds on the skill of paraphrasing and pays attention to the speaker's verbal and non-verbal responses. With reflecting feelings, the listener demonstrates sensitivity to unexpressed feelings, by using hunches and guesses. Even if the listener does not capture the exact feelings, the listener is showing effort to trying to understand the speaker's emotions.

Referring back to the earlier paraphrasing example with the resident and officer, reflecting feelings further strengthens a recognition that the officer is trying to "get" into the citizens shoes, rather than expressing how the officer might feel in the situation.

"You seem really annoyed and disappointed that the police never address this problem."

The citizen might then respond:

"I am not annoyed, I'm fed up!"

When an inaccurate reflection of feeling occurs, it prompts the speaker to correct the listener and further clarify his or her emotions. The listener's goal is always to identify the underlying feelings of the speaker, not the feelings of the listener.

Reflecting statements tend to be more effective than asking, "How did you feel?" Use, instead, the following phrasing:

"You feel worried because the fights seem to be upsetting for the kids."

"You <u>feel</u> scared <u>because</u> your sister may be involved in an unhealthy relationship."

Confronting surfaces as an essential skill for furthering a conversation, especially if the listener notices a discrepancy between a person's words and non-verbal behaviors.

It can be confusing to a listener to hear verbal content of a serious nature while the speaker is smiling. In conversation, one party might smile through a long and unpleasant description of an argument with coworkers.

The listener might observe:

"I'm confused. I notice you smiling while describing what seems to me to be an awful exchange with your office mate."

Here the listener provides feedback with the hope of aligning the conversation around congruent feelings.

Sometimes there are discrepancies between what a person is reporting in the moment and what a person recounts later:

"You said earlier this week that you paid the bill, but now you just said you didn't mail the check. Which is correct?"

Contradicting body language and verbal content or both can cause misunderstanding and obscure the real issue or message.

A helpful phrase to remember for the confronting skill is:

"On the one hand you tell me…on the other hand you tell me…"

Applied to a work setting issue, the supervisor might say:

"On the one hand you say you appreciate our conversation; on the other hand, your tone and body language tell me that you want it to end. Am I misreading you somehow?"

People often avoid the confronting skill because it can be challenging and uncomfortable to do. Yet, without its use, inconsistencies and misinterpretations can arise that negatively affect the conversation.

Concluding a Conversation

Clarifying   Summarizing

CHAPTER 3

Concluding a Conversation with Active Responding Skills

Conversations vary in purpose and duration. *Clarifying and summarizing* are two active responding skills that can help conclude a onetime exchange or an ongoing set of interactions. Understanding an entire conversation makes it more likely that both parties will know what happened, the impact of the dialogue, and if needed, what the next steps might be for future exchanges.

Clarifying includes statements to help the listener understand that the information shared is accurate to both parties in the conversation. One way to verbalize the clarification skill is:

"Let me make sure I have correctly heard what you said to me."

After the listener repeats the information, the speaker confirms or corrects the statement. Clarifying is a significant skill for all conversations, but especially in situations where someone, like a doctor, attorney, or business consultant, provides new and precise information that a person needs and wants to understand and retain.

Clarifying is also helpful when writing up a report to make sure that the information is correct. If the listener is confused, he or she could ask for more information by saying:

"I'm not quite sure I understand."

Often the clarifying skill will use a question:

"You say you are having headaches during the day. Can you tell me how often and how many?"

Clarifying helps ensure that the listener hears exactly what the speaker intends to be heard. In many situations, the reliability of report writing rests on the ability of the listener to gain and remember accurate information.

Clarifying can be very helpful when correcting employee behavior or policy violations. Clarifying allows for understanding between both parties on what created the issue, how the issue will be resolved, and the expected responsibilities of both parties.

Summarizing is a "recap" about what has transpired in a conversation as it ends. The listener uses the skills of focusing, paraphrasing, and clarifying to help summarize. Summarizing involves the use of:

"Do I have that right?"

For example, the listener might say:

"As we finish up our appointment today, it seems that though you're recovering on a physical level, there are several issues that continue to worry you, like how you will perform in your job or how others will see you. Is that correct?"

In this example, the objective is to give an individual a chance to clarify, correct, or elaborate upon content shared in the conversation. The use of summarizing confirms to others that their voice and ideas matter. Some conversations might end without summarizing, but in cases where there will be follow up interactions, summarizing is a skill to help link the current conversation to a future one.

Together clarifying and summarizing work in concert with each other to demonstrate that the listener is attending to the speaker in a wholehearted manner and is taking the time to make sure that messages sent to the listener are heard, reported back, and corrected, when necessary. All parties in a conversation can access these skills. The more people are proficient in active listening and responding skills the better the results of the interaction.

Essential Active Listening and Responding Skills

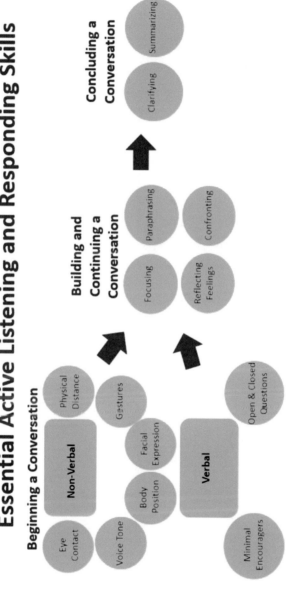

Sample Language for Active Listening and Responding

Beginning a Conversation	Building and Continuing a Conversation	Concluding a Conversation
Door Openers • "What's on your mind?" • "Tell me about your experience." • "Can you say more?" **Minimal Encouragers** • "I see." • "I hear you." • "I'm with you."	**Focusing** • "Let me pull this together a little." • "Let's stay with your description of what happened." **Paraphrasing** • "Your shift begins at 9:00 am, but you arrive ten minutes late and you don't see a problem." **Focusing and Paraphrasing** • "Let me make sure I understand: you are fed up with the deliveries being consistently late." **Reflecting Feelings** • "You feel worried because the policy changes are going to affect your job security." • "You are feeling anxious and frustrated because of all the obstacles in your way." **Confronting** • "You told me you handed in your homework, but your teacher called and said the homework was late."	**Clarifying** • "Let me make sure I have correctly heard what you said to me." • "I'm not quite sure I understand." **Summarizing** • "In our conversation today you identified the vehicle as a red Ford, gave a description of the suspect as a middle-aged white male, and stated that the burglary occurred at 8pm. Do I have that right?"

Active Listening and Responding

Skills Review

Being aware of our experiences when interacting with others at home, at work, in social situations, can increase understanding of how non-verbal and verbal skills enhance or hinder such interactions. Take a moment to review the questions below.

1. Think about the people you enjoy talking to and who you seek out when you have a problem, some positive news to share, or a question to ask:

- What draws you to these individuals?
- How would you describe their eye contact and body language?
- What do they do or say to help you feel comfortable and heard?
- How do you generally feel after speaking with these individuals?

2. Now, reflect on interactions you have had with people you do not enjoy talking with or you prefer to avoid altogether:

- What do these individuals do to push you away?
- How would you describe their eye contact and body language?

- What do they do and say that makes you feel uncomfortable, unimportant, or not heard?
- How do you generally feel after you encounter these individuals?

3. As you reflect on your answers for questions 1 and 2, give your definition of an effective listener.

4. Now shift to a focus on yourself. How would describe your

Eye Contact

- Stares
- Occasional
- Avoidant

Gestures

- Stiff
- Inviting
- Off-putting

Voice Tone

- Too loud
- Too soft
- Hesitant
- Soothing

Facial Expression

- Lack of interest or mask like
- Concern
- Angry

Physical Distance

- Very close
- Close
- Distant

Body Position

- Confident
- Aggressive
- Inviting
- Disinterested

Reviewing Assumptions and Responses

1. You ask to speak to a coworker and when this person walks into your office, he takes off his coat, loosens his tie, and puts his feet up on a chair:

- What assumptions do you make from his behavior?
- How might you respond?

2. You ask to meet with a student in your school to gather information on a classroom quarrel. The student sits as far away as she can from you, folds her arms, and looks over your head:

- What assumptions do you make from this behavior?
- How might you respond?

3. You walk into a shop in your town, no one speaks to you, and the sales personnel scowl and look away from you:

- What assumptions do you make from this behavior?
- How might you respond?

4. You work the reference desk at the university library. A student approaches your desk yelling at you about an overdue book charge:

- What assumptions do you make from this behavior?
- How might you respond?

Active Listening & Responding Skills: A Review

Basic Interpersonal Skills

(ME) Minimal encouragers   (RF) Reflecting feelings
(DO) Door openers   (Con) Confronting
(F) Focusing   (Clar) Clarifying
(P) Paraphrasing   (S) Summarizing

Directions: Match the letters of the skill above to appropriate phrase below:

1. "You seem annoyed that the police are not addressing this traffic problem." (   )

2. "Let me make sure I have correctly heard what you said to me." (   )

3. "Please hold on a second and tell me more about the description of the car." (   )

4. "Take your time and tell me what you want me to know about the accident." (   )

5. "You identified the vehicle, gave a description of the suspect, and told us what time the burglary occurred." (   )

6. "So, you are saying that many violations occur in your neighborhood and you don't see any police action." (   )

7. "I see, please tell me more." (   )

8. "On the one hand you said you were at the grocery store at 4pm; on the other hand, you were sighted at the movie theater at 4pm." (   )

51

PART TWO

Applying Active Listening and Responding Skills

to Giving and Receiving Feedback and

Facilitating Meetings and Other Task Groups

CHAPTER 4

Applying Active Listening and Responding Skills to Giving and Receiving Feedback

In the previous chapters, the reader learned basic active listening and responding skills that serve as the bridge to gaining competency in interpersonal civil discourse. In this chapter attention goes to an often-overlooked and misunderstood competency, that of giving and receiving positive and corrective feedback.

Positive feedback reinforces successful performance and builds confidence and self-esteem. *Corrective feedback* provides the receiver with directions and incentives to develop, improve, and change behaviors, and to achieve excellence.

Everyone receives feedback over the lifetime; however, most people avoid feedback, finding it too confrontational. These negative attitudes exist even though people want to know how they are perceived in the workplace and with family members and friends.

In our discussion, the term, *giver,* refers to the one delivering feedback. This person could be a supervisor, parent, teacher, community citizen, co-worker, sibling, spouse, police officer, or manager. The term, *receiver* refers to the recipient of feedback.

Most people do not like to give and receive feedback, especially feedback of a corrective nature because of many factors. Feedback givers often feel insecure about whether they have the skills to deliver feedback. They also worry about upsetting others (Hulse-Killacky & Page, 1994). Those receiving feedback frequently interpret the feedback as a negative statement about their personal worth. Put together these and other emotional, cultural, and familial attitudes produce formidable obstacles.

In 1983, Irvin Yalom wrote that interpersonal feedback is an uncommon transaction in our culture. While his words resonate today, it is also true that the ability to give and receive feedback is an indicator of civil and productive interpersonal communication. Thus, it is incumbent on all of us to strive for ways to address obstacles to giving and receiving feedback and to figure out how to make feedback exchange more attractive, acceptable, and doable.

This chapter has several goals:

- To introduce Preplanning for Feedback as a key competency for addressing barriers and normalizing interpersonal feedback for both the giver and receiver

- To introduce the Corrective Feedback Instrument-Revised (CFI-R) as a tool to implement preplanning

- To introduce the Cycle of Effective Feedback as a guide for giving and processing feedback

- To emphasize throughout how the intentional use of active listening and responding skills, presented in chapters 1, 2, and 3 helps create a climate to support effective feedback exchange for the giver and receiver

Preplanning for Interpersonal Feedback

The Purpose of Preplanning

Because feedback exchange is complex, and no two people are likely to experience the same reactions and concerns, *preplanning* for feedback surfaces as an important proficiency to master to pave the way for interpersonal feedback. Particularly in work and educational settings, preplanning for feedback helps those being supervised shift from avoiding feedback as a statement of personal criticism to reframing feedback as a tool to enhance learning and promote development. Additionally, preplanning for feedback instills confidence in the feedback giver and helps both the feedback giver and receiver build and strengthen a relationship to support feedback exchange (Hulse & Robert, 2014).

When the goal is to help those receiving feedback progress into valuable members of a company or group, then feedback becomes more relevant and rewarding and improves workplace and group interactions. When delivered by a person with active listening and responding skills the receiver is less likely to misunderstand the feedback's purpose. Thoughtful preplanning on the part of the feedback giver helps reduce receivers' beliefs that they are being harassed or discriminated against because of gender, age, or culture.

Parents use feedback on a regular basis to teach their children, help them develop decision making skills, to learn right from wrong, and understand behavioral guidelines. The act of giving ongoing parental feedback is reflexive and continuous. Active listening and responding skills will improve this never ending parental responsibility.

In the workplace however, feedback can be inconsistent or nonexistent. When the need arises for feedback, it often comes across as unwelcome, contentious or disciplinary. The consistent use of active listening and responding skills will help create an organizational culture that supports corrective feedback as a developmental process, rather than a punitive one. Supervisors will gain a better sense of their responsibilities and how to accomplish them and receivers will feel valued and rewarded for performance. If feedback becomes commonplace, then it can transform the culture of the organization.

Steps to Implement Preplanning

Corrective Feedback Instrument-Revised (CFI-R)

The CFI-R was developed primarily to encourage preplanning conversations between the giver and receiver with the goal of increasing an understanding of the receiver's feelings and reactions to corrective feedback. Designed initially for those who facilitate feedback in groups the CFI-R has broad utility to any interaction between a feedback giver and receiver. Review of items on the CFI-R helps the giver and receiver uncover and discuss potential barriers to giving and receiving feedback.

The CFI-R consists of 30 items, presented in a 6-point Likert format of response choices, strongly disagree, disagree, slightly disagree, slightly agree, agree, and strongly agree. Items load on one of six factors that together provide comprehensive information on a person's reactions to giving, receiving, and clarifying corrective feedback. This information helps the giver and receiver identify and explore a range of feelings, thoughts, and preferences to inform the feedback giver's method of delivery that is likely to work best for the receiver.

The original instrument published in 1994 (Hulse-Killacky & Page) and the revised instrument (Hulse-Killacky, Orr, & Paradise, 2006) have been used widely to encourage conversations between givers and receivers to discuss and normalize the actual implementation of corrective feedback and enhance the giver-receiver relationship. When a relationship of mutual understanding and respect exists between the giver and receiver then interpersonal feedback is poised for success (Alexander & Hulse-Killacky, 2005; Hulse, & Robert, 2014; McDermott & Hulse, 2012).

In the following pages we present two helpful preplanning methods derived from the CFI-R:

- The CFI-R Items Matched by Factors
- The CFI-R Short Form

As a warm-up to each method the giver can initiate a conversation with the receiver on the following questions:

When someone says, "I want to give you some feedback," ask yourself, what do you think, what do you feel, what do you do, what are your concerns?

When you give someone corrective feedback, what do you think, what do you feel, what do you do, what are your concerns?

A brief discussion of the receiver's responses guides the giver's next preplanning steps.

CFI-R Items Matched by Factors. The **thirty** CFI-R items are organized around six factors: *Leader, Feeling, Evaluative, Childhood Memories, Written, and Clarifying.* Each factor represents a content theme. The giver can ask the receiver to rate all or some of the items from strongly disagree, disagree, slightly disagree, slightly agree, agree, or strongly agree. These ratings assist the giver in gaining an understanding the receiver's feelings and thoughts about corrective feedback.

Leader Factor: This factor includes **seven** items that emphasize the responsibility of the feedback giver to establish norms supporting the exchange of corrective feedback. After all, the giver is the one responsible for setting the stage for interpersonal feedback.

- *When the norms of the group support the exchange of corrective feedback, I will be open to receiving corrective feedback*

- *I like to hear the leader clearly state his or her support for corrective feedback*

- *If I am in a group setting where corrective feedback exchange has been established as a norm, I will be receptive to corrective feedback*

- *If I observed the leader reinforcing the giving of corrective feedback in the group, I would be willing to give corrective feedback more frequently*

- *If I have a part in helping set norms for receiving corrective feedback, then I will probably be open to receiving corrective feedback*

- *I believe that positive experiences with corrective feedback can occur in a group when the leader takes an active role in setting the stage*

- *If I can take part in helping to set norms for giving corrective feedback, I will probably be more open to giving corrective feedback*

Feeling Factor: This factor captures the range of emotions and feelings associated with giving and receiving corrective feedback. Responses to the **five** items help the feedback giver better comprehend the feelings of the receiver.

- *Telling someone I have a different view is scary to me*

- *Verbalizing corrective feedback is awkward for me*

- *I try to avoid being in conflict with others whenever possible*

- *Most of the time I am too uncomfortable to say what I really mean to someone else*

- *I worry too much about upsetting others when I have to give corrective feedback*

Evaluative Factor: This factor includes **five** items that concentrate on themes of criticism and evaluation. One of the challenges to hearing and accepting feedback is the belief that feedback is a statement about one's personal value. The receiver's responses to these items can reveal where future barriers to hearing feedback may lie.

- *I feel criticized when I receive corrective feedback*

- *I think negative thoughts about myself when I receive corrective feedback*

- *It is hard for me not to interpret corrective feedback as a criticism of my personal competence*

- *When I receive corrective feedback, I think I have failed in some way*

- *When I am given corrective feedback, I think my skills are being questioned*

Childhood Memories Factor: The **six** items on this factor call attention to how many reactions to feedback can begin during one's early years; forming memories that become obstacles to receiving feedback later on. While memories of early experiences may not predict a receiver's current behavior, responses to these items can provide the giver with additional insight into how the receiver feels about giving and receiving corrective feedback.

- *I remember corrective feedback delivered as a child to be critical*

- *Because my childhood memories of corrective feedback are negative ones, I am very sensitive about receiving corrective feedback now*

- *Receiving corrective feedback as a child was painful for me*

- *I fear conflict because of my negative experiences with corrective feedback as a child*

- *When I reflect on the corrective feedback I received as a child, I hesitate to give others corrective feedback*

- *I always felt criticized whenever I received corrective feedback as a child*

Written Feedback Factor: These **four** items provide the giver information on the receiver's preferences for written or spoken feedback. Some people prefer feedback in written form; others prefer to receive feedback verbally. The giver can use the receiver's responses to decide on using written or verbal feedback, or a mix of both kinds.

- *Giving written corrective feedback is easier for me to do than speaking directly to the person*

- *When I need to give corrective feedback, I prefer to write it out*

- *I prefer to receive corrective feedback in written form*

- *It is easier for me to write down my corrective feedback than to speak it*

Clarifying Feedback Factor: The **three** items on this factor highlight the need for clarification so that all parties understand the message sent. One of the missed opportunities in feedback exchange is taking the necessary time to make sure that the receiver has heard and understood the message and knows what to do next. Often, the giver may need to directly ask the receiver if he or she comprehends the intended feedback message.

- *I am usually too uncomfortable to ask someone to clarify corrective feedback delivered to me*

- *When I am not sure about the corrective feedback message delivered to me I do not ask for clarification*

- *It is too scary for me to ask other group members to clarify their corrective feedback if it is unclear to me*

Responses to the CFI-R Items Matched with Factors yield a wealth of information to explore. When both giver and receiver complete the items, there is even more information available to potentially aid both parties. By employing a range of non-verbal and verbal active listening and responding skills, the giver further enhances the likelihood that a preplanning conversation will begin to demystify worries about feedback and strengthen the giver-receiver relationship.

The CFI-R Short Form

In this condensed version of the CFI-R, the feedback giver asks the receiver to rate the **eleven** items below from strongly disagree, disagree, slightly disagree, slightly agree, agree, or strongly agree. These items derive from the Childhood Memories and Evaluative factors. The selection of these specific items comes from research findings suggesting that a focus on early recollections about feedback paired with one's personal assessment of the evaluative nature of feedback, will come together to help the giver identify barriers to receiving and applying feedback (Stroud, Olguin, & Marley, 2016). For example, if the receiver agrees that she remembers corrective feedback as punitive or painful and that she currently thinks negative thoughts when she receives corrective feedback, then the giver will want to carefully explore these responses with her to learn where the most opposition to corrective feedback exists.

CFI-R Short Form (Items from Childhood Memories and Evaluative Factors)

1. I always felt criticized whenever I received corrective feedback as a child

2. I feel criticized when I receive corrective feedback

3. I remember corrective feedback delivered as a child to be critical

4. I think negative thoughts about myself when I receive corrective feedback

5. Because my childhood memories of corrective feedback are negative ones, I am very sensitive about receiving corrective feedback now

6. It is hard for me not to interpret corrective feedback as a criticism of my personal competence

7. Receiving corrective feedback as a child was painful for me

8. When I receive corrective feedback, I think I have failed in some way

9. I fear conflict because of my negative experiences with corrective feedback as a child

10. When I am given corrective feedback, I think my skills are being questioned

11. When I reflect on the corrective feedback I received as a child, I hesitate to give others corrective feedback

In order to keep the conversation going the giver applies the full range of active listening and responding skills. For example, the receiver might strongly agree with:

"I feel criticized when I receive corrective feedback" and *"I think negative thoughts about myself when I receive corrective feedback."*

The giver could observe:

"I noticed on your responses to the CFI-R Short Form that you equate corrective feedback to criticism. Because you will receive corrective feedback from me throughout this training period, I want us to talk about how I can make the feedback experience helpful for you.

Benefits of Preplanning for Feedback

Preplanning for feedback is an essential competency for the giver to master. When the giver intentionally takes time to build a relationship with the receiver, feedback becomes a source of learning for the receiver, rather than a noxious event to resist and avoid.

When the giver completes the CFI-R items, along with the receiver, more information is available to highlight potential differences. For example, the giver may not rate corrective feedback as critical; however, the receiver might feel criticized when receiving corrective feedback and thus hold a dissimilar reaction. Those in positions to deliver positive and corrective feedback need to focus on what works best for the receiver, not on what the giver agrees with or prefers. Preplanning offers a way to address this task.

Cycle of Effective Feedback:
Sequential Steps to Follow When Delivering Feedback

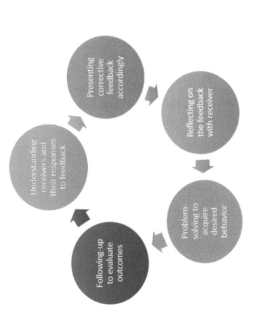

Activating the Cycle of Effective Feedback

With knowledge and understanding gained through the preplanning process, the feedback giver is ready to shift to the five steps in the *Cycle of Effective Feedback*. Non-verbal and verbal active listening and responding skills provide language to support implementation.

> **Step one**: As discussed in the preplanning section, *Understanding* the receiver helps the giver maximize success moving forward. Learning the meaning behind the receiver's responses to CFI-R items helps build a relationship and provides the giver with important information.

> Use of appropriate non-verbal and verbal attending skills by the giver builds and enhances understanding. Focusing, paraphrasing, reflecting feelings, confronting, and summarizing assist the giver in gaining a sense of how the receiver interprets and responds to feedback.

Step two: The next step in the cycle is *presenting* feedback. To illustrate, a bank manager observes that an employee's voice tone and general attending behaviors convey disrespect to a customer. She might say, "I noticed that your voice tone was harsh and rude. Let's talk about what happened, how you were feeling, and what your next steps might be to improve your future exchanges with customers."

Once again, non-verbal and verbal attending skills join with focusing, paraphrasing, reflecting feelings, and summarizing to make sure the feedback giver is able to effectively communicate those observations to the person receiving her feedback.

Step three: The third step in the cycle involves *reflecting* on the feedback. With previous information on the receiver's reactions to feedback as reported on the CFI-R, the bank manager wants to make sure that the receiver has accurately heard her feedback. "I want you to tell me what you heard me say to you about the interaction with the bank customer." How the receiver responds can inform what happens next. Perhaps the manager needs to repeat and better clarify her corrective feedback so the receiver can truly understand the feedback message and translate the message to future actions.

Minimal encouragers and door openers combine with reflecting feelings, clarifying, and summarizing to make sure that the receiver hears and reflects back the intended message from the feedback giver.

Step four: Once the receiver accurately reflects on the feedback, the manager can observe the receiver's next interaction at work. This step refers to *problem solving*. The receiver's behavior in a future encounter with a bank customer will validate if the receiver heard the feedback and knows how to implement the feedback. The giver will be looking for evidence of positive behavioral change, some change, or no change.

In this step, the feedback giver employs a range of skills such as, focusing, reflecting feelings, confronting, clarifying, and summarizing.

Step five: At this point in the cycle and based on the degree of change on the part of the receiver, the bank manager may use the *following-up* step to revisit previous steps in the cycle to practice the desired behavior, or move to another performance area.

Use of all the non-verbal and verbal active listening and responding skills come together to help the giver complete step five.

The Centrality of Active Listening and Responding Skills in Giving and Receiving Feedback

Activing listening and responding skills employed in a thoughtful, planned manner and in conjunction with a tool like the CFI-R can help overcome obstacles to hearing, accepting and applying feedback. Talking through the feedback receiver's anxieties is an essential first step in normalizing feedback as a worthwhile activity. Taking time to figure out each person's position on feedback can help the receiver listen to the feedback and make recommended changes, rather than pushing the feedback away and shutting down the learning process.

Throughout life, people give and receive feedback on a daily basis in families, in schools, and at work. The more people gain competencies in effective ways to give and receive feedback as methods for learning and improving, and achieving excellence, then the entire culture benefits. Active listening and responding skills serve as an important competency for making feedback exchange an

achievable opportunity, instead of a perceived obligation

from which to escape.

CHAPTER 5

Applying Active Listening and Responding Skills to Facilitating Meetings and Other Task Groups

Attention shifts in this chapter to another set of competencies requiring a strong baseline of interpersonal skills. Facilitating the work of two or more individuals gathered together for the purposes of problem solving, classroom learning, task completion, staff meetings, to name a few, requires mastery of active listening and responding skills and an array of other skills specific to working with people in group settings.

Meetings, often characterized as boring, unproductive, and a waste of time, generally receive bad press. One of the challenges for a facilitator is managing members' varied personal communication styles and specific expectations and goals. If a person gains leadership status in business, church, volunteer agency, hospital, police department, or school settings, that person can expect to facilitate meetings or teams as part of the job description.

Given that most people dread meetings, there are good reasons for facilitators to learn how to shape these types of interpersonal encounters into civil and productive exchanges that successfully accomplish goals.

The purpose of this chapter is to introduce concepts and competencies, that combined with the intentional application of non-verbal and verbal active listening and responding skills can help facilitators and members alike improve the outcomes and reputation of meetings and task groups. Meetings often fail because members do not feel welcomed, engaged, listened to, understood, and made to feel that their investment of time and effort leads to satisfying results.

In this chapter the reader will:

- Learn and understand the concepts of **process** and **content** which serve as the foundation for effective meetings

- Learn a movement activity that can identify member personal preferences in order to build knowledge, understanding, and empathy among all participants

- Learn basic phases of a meeting in order to accomplish tasks and engage member participation

- Learn sample language to apply active listening and responding skills, presented in chapters 1, 2, and 3, to a set of leadership competencies that help the task group succeed

Process and Content

Process in meetings refers to interpersonal relationships; how individuals interact with each other to get the job accomplished. Facilitators need to get to know their members in order to recognize and respond to behaviors that can enhance or hinder the work of a meeting. Most people think that meetings are all about content. Without attention to process, or the dynamics of people in the room, meetings will fail. When facilitators attend to process, they maximize the likelihood that their meetings will be productive for all present. (Hulse-Killacky, Killacky & Donigian, 2001) Process addresses the questions, "Who am I? Who am I with you? Who are we together?"

Content in meetings is easier to define. Content refers to the purpose or reason for the meeting. One of the complaints about meetings is that they do not accomplish anything. Thus, facilitators need a plan to ensure that the members work together to define and accomplish stated goals. Content addresses the questions, "What do we have to do? How will we get it done?"

The balance of Process and Content is the facilitator's responsibility (Hulse Killacky et al, 2001; McDermott, & Hulse, October, 2012). It is easy to fall into the content trap, find a solution, and end the meeting. Attention to process requires a focus on the most important factor in the meeting, the people. When facilitators ignore the people in the room and their potential contributions to the task and the advancement of teamwork, they lose an opportunity to galvanize the efforts of all those present. Keeping process in mind allows facilitators to focus on, evaluate, and manage the skills of the people, while encouraging all to share in the meeting's accomplishments. When group members feel valued as fully engaged participants in the purpose of the meeting, they will freely contribute. When facilitators utilize the competencies of cutting off and drawing out, all members have the chance to share their voice and listen to others.

Facilitators must understand that how they observe and respond to members' non-verbal and verbal behaviors influences outcomes. Meetings have the potential to be effective when facilitators pay attention to the people in the room and apply methods for engaging everyone's voices.

Building Member to Member Interaction

A significant first step for facilitators is to address potential roadblocks by helping members get to know one another in order to increase member-to-member interaction. Why is this important? Members enter any group situation with their own perspectives and preferences. Once uncovered and discussed, members have an opportunity to form working relationships that honor their similarities and differences. Left alone, these differences may arise and obstruct interactions. One helpful preplanning intervention is based on the Myers-Briggs Instrument (Briggs, 1987). In this activity the facilitator invites members to move to a position on each of the following four dimensions that most accurately represents them in most situations. With the use of active listening and responding skills, the facilitator engages members in a discussion of their placement and the implications of learning about self and others. This activity helps members gain knowledge about themselves and become aware that others' perspectives may differ from their own perspectives.

Exploring Personal Preferences

- *Some people prefer to talk things out; others prefer to think things through*

- *Some people prefer to have the specifics; others prefer to work with the big picture*

- *Some people prefer to hear logical implications behind making a decision; others prefer to know the impact that a decision has on people*

- *Some people prefer to come to a conclusion and finish a task; others prefer to stay open to options and not come to a decision too quickly*

Facilitators might ask members as they choose their positions to reflect on their personal preferences:

Bill, please talk about why you placed yourself as someone who prefers specifics. Why do you think that is important for us all to know about you?

Mary, you chose the big picture. How do you think your choice will play out as we work together on our task?

Bob as a new member of this team, how might the differences expressed by Bill and Mary help or hinder the work in our meetings? How might those differences influence your actions in the meeting?

Use of *minimal encouragers* like:

"Tell me more"

***paraphrasing* statements like:**

"You have always worked best when you knew what was specifically expected of you," and

 ***reflecting feelings*:**

"Mary, you are most comfortable with big picture ideas,"

are examples of the application of fundamental active listening and responding skills to the processing of this group activity.

There are several practical benefits to bringing common sources of conflict and difference into the open. Members appreciate being able to clarify their own viewpoints and perspectives and listen to those of other members. This type of structured dialog helps increase the chances that in time all members will fully participate in the meeting and learn from each other, which can only strengthen successful outcomes.

The Beginning, the Middle, and the End

Meetings have a beginning, a middle point, and an end. Knowing the function of each phase helps facilitators balance attention to the purpose of the meeting, as they make sure to stay tuned to the interpersonal dynamics expressed by members. (Hulse-Killacky et al, 2001)

In the bell-shaped visual below, one sees how a meeting progresses through the beginning, middle, and end phases. Sample language is introduced to initiate each phase. One also sees how the bolded process line supports the content line. This illustration reinforces the principle that *attention to process* (the relationships in the meeting) is essential to achieving the *content* (or purpose) of the meeting.

In the *beginning* phase, facilitators check in with all members, clarify the purpose of the day's meeting, and invite each member's participation. The *middle* phase represents the part of the meeting where members focus on the task to accomplish or the purpose of the meeting. The *end* phase refers to the often overlooked part of the meeting where everyone devotes enough time to wrap up the work and decide on next steps. A facilitator's responsibility is to monitor these phases and to make sure to sequence activities so that the meeting begins and ends on time.

Facilitating Phases of a Meeting

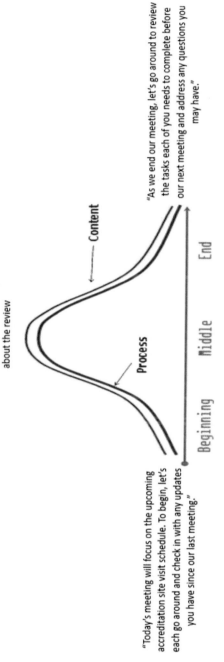

"Bob, I need to stop you. I want to get back to what John was saying about the schedule with the director before we move on to your point about the review"

Content

Process

"Today's meeting will focus on the upcoming accreditation site visit schedule. To begin, let's each go around and check in with any updates you have since our last meeting."

"As we end our meeting, let's go around to review the tasks each of you needs to complete before our next meeting and address any questions you may have."

Beginning   Middle   End

Leadership Competencies

Leadership competencies in the next chart represent the bread and butter of effective meetings and other task groups. While important to facilitators, these competencies are equally valuable to members. After all, most people participate as members of meetings more often than they facilitate meetings, so it makes sense for facilitators and members to learn these competencies to enhance the experience for everyone. For example, there may be times when members have to jump in and take the lead. The basic learning point here is that meetings work best when all participants engage.

In the discussion of leadership competencies below, one sees how non-verbal and verbal active listening and responding skills contribute to the application of these competencies (Jacobs, Masson, Harvill & Schimmel, 2012).

Rounds build member participation and help gather information. Rounds are a quick way to circle the room and hear from everyone. The facilitator may want to use a round to check in with all participants, stop to clarify how the group is going at mid-point, and near the end, summarize accomplishments and plan for next steps. Understanding the intent of rounds will guide the facilitator's use of this helpful technique.

Cutting Off represents an essential competency in the facilitator's toolbox. Often avoided as a harsh and unfriendly action, this competency can actually assist in the work of the group. How many times have members endured rambling or extraneous conversation to a point where they shut down and disengage from the group?

Paired with an inviting tone of voice and the skill of focusing, the facilitator could say,

"Jane, because of our time constraints today and the need to gather input from everyone, I want to hear from other members. Then I will check in again with you."

Holding the Focus and Shifting the Focus are additional competencies that assist the facilitator in sequencing the meeting and making sure that those in the meeting get to address the significant topics for the day. There are times in meetings where it is necessary to stick with the topic under discussion, to **hold the focus**, or when it is time to move on, to **shift the focus** to another topic of significance.

Drawing Out is a competency used to engage less vocal members. Voice tone and eye contact help the facilitator attend to the quiet member. Sometimes facilitators shy away from this skill so as not to seem pushy. Yet, in interpersonal settings, success of the meeting occurs through having access to all voices. A facilitator might say to the group as a whole,

"I would like to hear from each of you as to your reason for being in this meeting today."

Later on, the facilitator could add,

"I have not heard from you today, Mary. What do you think about our planned protocol?"

Often present in business meetings there is an organizational hierarchy. A member may be reluctant to participate as a result of a perceived power differential. It is the facilitator's duty to get everyone involved. Hidden treasures and new ideas are found when everyone contributes. Many times after meetings, the grumbling begins, often from members who have not participated for various reasons. This type of behavior casts a negative perception on the meeting. Drawing out during meetings is a preventative tool that encourages all members to participate.

Here-and-Now is probably one of the most effective ways to enhance the work of a group. Here-and-now refers to being fully present and attentive to non-verbal and verbal actions in a meeting that can interrupt or stall the work. Suppose a member grimaces when another member speaks. What can a facilitator do?

The point of the here-and-now is to call out the "elephant in the room." In the above example, if left unacknowledged the member's unspoken disagreement will negatively affect the productivity of the group. Use of the confronting skill presented in chapter 2 and "I" statements can assist. Here-and-now observations take courage as well.

A facilitator observes a change in the level of interaction and says,

"I notice that when we were discussing pay raises everyone participated in the conversation. Now that we have shifted to a focus on workloads I detect very little input. Let's go around the table so I can hear from each of you on this topic."

Rounds

- Quick method for:
  - Checking in with participants at the beginning, middle, and end of a meeting
  - Building member participation
  - Gathering information
  - Checking in on how the meeting is progressing
  - Summarizing learning points from the meeting
  - Planning for next steps

Cutting Off

- Skill used to break up rambling or extraneous conversation in a meeting.
- This is a skill that is uncomfortable for many people because they think cutting off is rude.

Holding the Focus and Shifting the Focus

- Cutting off is needed to help **hold the focus** on a topic of importance in the meeting or **shift the focus** to another topic that is important to the purpose of the meeting.

Drawing out

- This is an important skill for engaging less vocal participants in a meeting so that all participants' voices are heard in conversation.

Here-and-Now

- Paying attention to what is happening and how things are happening is a great tool for facilitating meetings.
- Non-verbal behaviors in a meeting are often indicators of events that need to be addressed.

Sample Language for Balancing Process and Content in Meetings

The following sample language chart provides options for facilitators to use to address process and content issues during various phases of the meeting. Having sample language to practice with can build confidence in facilitators and members, and ensure that the meeting works for all present.

Sample Language for Balancing Process and Content in Meetings

Beginning	Middle	End
Opening Round • "Our purpose today is to review the schedule for the upcoming accreditation visit and your representation for the event." • "To get started, I'd like for each of you to bring us up to date on any professional initiatives." • "Let's start with a quick check-in; are you here, not here, getting here?"	**Cutting Off and Holding the Focus** • "Bob, I need to stop you. I want to get back to what John was saying before we move on to your reaction." **Drawing Out** • "I haven't heard from you yet, Mary. What do you think about our planned site visit?" **Shifting the Focus** • "I am aware that we have 15 minutes left in our meeting and we haven't finalized the schedule yet. I would like us to move on to that topic." **Addressing Here and Now Behavior** • "I need to stop the meeting for a moment to check in with how all of you are reacting to Bob's comment on the schedule."	**Closing Round** • "As a result of our conversation today, I would like each of you to summarize your roles during the site visit." • "To finish up today, let's go around and say what we will be bringing to our next meeting before the accreditation team arrives."

The Centrality of Active Listening and Responding Skills for Effective Meetings

This chapter focused on the application of active listening and responding skills to specific concepts and competencies that help make meetings and other task groups effective and meaningful. Meetings do not succeed by content alone. Attention to the people in the room and their needs, expectations, and preferences, requires facilitators to learn ways to engage and welcome members so they want to be present and contribute to the success of the meeting.

The interplay between leadership competencies and non-verbal and verbal active listening and responding skills demonstrates how valuable they can be in meetings and other task groups. With practice and intentionality, meetings can become places of good work, accomplishment, and satisfying interpersonal relationships.

PART THREE

A Call to Action

CHAPTER 6

A Call to Action for Interpersonal Relationships and the Skills to Listen and Respond

Throughout *#CanWeTalk*, interpersonal relationships are outlined as essential to human existence. The skewed nature of communication evident in today's digital age creates a deficit in people's ability to call forth active listening and responding skills, which help them learn about one another, begin to understand one another, and eventually develop empathy for differing perspectives. Once relegated to the background as soft skills, the ability to demonstrate solid listening skills is slowly moving into the forefront of discussions about how to be successful in work and life. In short, active listening is a first step to building civil human interactions that permeate every aspect of one's existence.

#CanWeTalk presented a set of basic skills and ways to use the skills to improve and strengthen civil discourse and interpersonal relationships at home, at work, and in social and civic interactions. Ivey, Ivey, and Zalaquette (2016) cite research supporting how the skills of paraphrasing, reflecting feelings and summarizing help make a relationship work. Mental health providers use listening as the key competency to engage their clients and to help them open up to disclose important information. These same skills and outcomes are available to all of us in all of our interactions if we take the time to learn and master them. It is logical to believe that most people will open up and share feelings and information when others listen to them in a genuine manner.

According to Lolly Daskel (2017), there are five basic emotional intelligence skills that cannot be automated or outsourced, and which will never go out of style.

1. *Knowing one's feelings, strengths, and weaknesses, and how one's actions and emotions affect others*

2. *Building and maintaining interpersonal relationships that support humans' needs for social interaction and friendship*

3. *Recognizing that successful communication requires a speaker and a listener and the skills to demonstrate wholehearted active listening skills*

4. *Being able to demonstrate empathy which is a building block for building trust and a key element for effective leadership*

5. *Understanding that effective feedback exchange will always require a person-to-person connection in order to inspire real growth and development*

Mastery of active listening and responding skills is crucial in order to achieve the level of emotional intelligence Daskel describes. If a safe environment is a goal then voice tone, gestures, and style of eye contact are keys to building a climate of safety. In many situations, the listener must make conscious moment-to-moment decisions in response to the verbal and emotional responses of others. Mastery of active listening and responding skills helps prepare for this task. Active listening and responding skills strengthen chances that the listener will be able to express his or her sensitivity to the emotions of others and demonstrate an ability to see another's vision of the world.

Empathy is key to bridging individual differences. The expression of emotional empathy communicates an understanding of one's emotions; the expression of cognitive empathy conveys the listener's ability to understand the motivation of others (Ivey et al., 2016). Confronting, reframing, and reflecting meaning within a climate of trust and safety can result in productive actions to support the needs of the person speaking.

Material covered in *#CanWeTalk* reaches far into the common everyday exchanges people have with family members, friends, co-workers, and supervisors, and others at community events, PTA meetings, church gatherings, faculty meetings, sports events, and neighborhood groups. The goal throughout is a call to action to increase proficiency in building civil and engaged human interactions.

One's ingenuity will guide the reader forward. For example,

> **A middle school teacher** can select several skills from chapters 1, 2, and 3 to offer a short training module in the classroom to teach students to use the skills of focusing, paraphrasing, and reflecting feelings in their daily interactions.

A manager of a health care facility can offer short training sessions on the impact and importance of non-verbal and verbal attending skills for staff in the reception office.

Newly promoted police sergeants can learn how to apply the active listening and responding skills to their tasks as supervisors who provide positive and corrective feedback to recruits and officers.

Organizational leaders can use active listening and responding skills to balance process and content in their meetings to communicate to all participants that their voices are welcomed and valued.

Medical schools can require training in active listening and responding skills to foster open and engaging communication between providers and patients. As Dr. Bernard Lown observed, "attentive listening is itself therapeutic" (1996, p.9).

The skill competencies presented in *#CanWeTalk* underscore the relevance of face to face conversation and are available to everyone to study, learn, and practice. People respond to words and gestures that bring them closer to others, to relieve their pain or anxieties, to build excitement and joy. Conversely, words can also cause one to feel worse and become demoralized. A disconnect with others can lead to feelings of loneliness that can become debilitating and eventually negatively affect one's physical health (Cacioppo & Patricin, 2008). Everyone needs human interactions and human relationships. Basic active listening and responding skills provide the direction and means to realize these needs.

There is much to do.

Let's get to work

Postscript

In his opinion piece in the Sunday, June 24, 2018 *New York Times,* Clay Routledge wrote that suicides are up 25% in the United States since 1999, across most ethnic and age groups. He presents several compelling reasons for this increase including people's need for meaning, and changes in the culture that result in more detachment and diminished feelings of belonging.

Routledge notes that "close relationships with other people are our greatest existential resource," which he believes serves as a passageway to meaning and purpose. He reports that across all demographics people see their most personally meaningful experiences to involve loved ones. He also maintains that people need to feel valued to believe that what they do matters and that they are making important contributions to a world that matters.

In his discussion of changes in the social landscape of America, Routledge observes that people are less likely today to know and interact with neighbors and to have access to individuals they can confide in and trust.

Talking and building human interactions with others is one way to increase the occurrence of neighborliness. The active listening and responding skills explored in *#CanWeTalk* provide each of us with tools to bridge the loneliness divide. As Cacioppo (2008) reminds us,

> "Feelings of social connection as well as feelings of disconnection, have an enormous influence on our bodies as well as our behaviors. We all decline physically sooner or later, but loneliness can increase the angle of the downward slope. Conversely, healthy connection can help slow that decline. Once we move into the realm of "high in social well-being" - and this is possible for any of us – we benefit from positive, restorative effects that can help keep us going longer and stronger" (p. 12).

Learning and mastering basic active listening and responding skills to bring us into closer and meaningful personal contact with one another is a step we can all take and is worth our time and effort.

Works Cited

Alexander, A., & Hulse-Killacky, D. (2005). Childhood memories and receptivity to corrective feedback in group supervision: Implications for group work. *Journal for Specialists in Group Work, 30,* 23-45.

Briggs, K. C. (1987*). Myers-Briggs type indicator.* Form G. Palo Alto, CA: Consulting Psychologists Press.

Cacioppo, J. T., & Patricin, W. (2008). *Human Nature and the Need for Social Connection.* New York, NY: W.W. Norton & Company, Inc.

Daskal, L. (2017). 6 emotional-intelligence job skills everyone will need in the next few years. Retrieved from https://www.inc.com/lolly-daskal/6-emotional-intelligence-job-skills-youll-need-in-.html?cid=search

Dyson, M. E. (2018). *What Truth Sounds Like. RFK, James Baldwin, and Our Unfinished Conversation about Race in America.* New York: St. Martin's Press.

Hatfield, T. (2018) *Truman 1.* Washington D.C.: Library of Congress.

Hulse-Killacky, D., & Page, B.J. (1994). Development of the Corrective Feedback Instrument: A tool for use in counselor training groups. *Journal for Specialists in Group Work, 19,* 197-210.

Hulse-Killacky, D., Killacky, J., & Donigian, J. (2001). *Making task groups work in your world.* Prentice Hall/Merrill.

Hulse-Killacky, D., Orr, J. & Paradise, L. (2006). The Corrective Feedback Instrument Revised. *Journal for Specialists in Group Work, 31,* 263-281.

Hulse, D., & Robert, T. (2014). Preplanning for feedback in clinical supervision: Enhancing readiness for feedback exchange. *The Journal for Counselor Preparation and Supervision, 6 (2).* http://dx.doi.org/10.7729/52.1091.

Ivey, A.E., Ivey, M.B., Zalaquett, C. (2016). The Neuroscience of Listening, Microskills and Empathy. *Counseling Today, 59(2),* 18-21. Alexandria, VA: American Counseling Association.

Jacobs, E.E., Masson, R.L., Harvill, R.L., Schimmel, C.J. (2012). *Group Counseling Strategies and Skills.* Belmont, CA: Brooks/Cole.

Joseph, R. (February 25, 2018). Doctors, Revolt! *New York Times*, p. SR12.

Lown, B. (1996). *The Lost Art of Healing. Practicing Compassion in Medicine.* New York: Ballantine Books.

McDermott, P. J., & Hulse, D. (February, 2012). Interpersonal skills training in police academy curriculum. *FBI Law Enforcement Bulletin, 81(2),* 16-20.

McDermott, P. J., & Hulse, D. (October, 2012). Strengthening police organizations through interpersonal leadership. *FBI Law Enforcement Bulletin, 81(10),* 19-23.

McDermott, P. J., & Hulse, D. (June, 2012). Corrective feedback in police work. *FBI Law Enforcement Bulletin, 81(6),* 13-17.

McDermott, P. J., & Hulse, D. (2014). *Policing in the 21st century: TALK trumps technology.* Santa Anna, CA: Police and Fire Publishing

McDermott, P. J., & Hulse, D. (November, 2016). Learning the art of active listening and responding: An ethical imperative for police training. *The Police Chief, 83 (11),* 26-31.

Okun, B., & Kantrowitz, R. E. (2015). Effective Helping: Interviewing and Counseling Techniques (8th ed). Cengage Learning.

Rogers, K. (July-August, 2018). Do your employees feel respected? *Harvard Business Review,* 62-71.

Routledge, C. (June 24, 2018). Suicides Have Increased. Is This an Existential Crisis? *New York Times,* p. SR 9.

Stroud, D., Olguin, D., & Marley, S. (2016). Relationship between counseling students' childhood memories and current negative self-evaluations when receiving corrective feedback. *International Journal for the Advancement of Counselling, 38(3),* 237-248.

Yalom, I.D., 1983, *In-Patient Group Psychotherapy* New York, NY: Basic Books.

Young, M. E. (2017). *Learning the Art of Helping: Building Blocks and Techniques (6th. Edition).* New York: Pearson/the Merrill Counseling Series.

Made in the USA
Middletown, DE
19 July 2019